The Frozen Mask

A Collection of Poems on Living with Parkinson's Disease

by
Denis Murphy

The Frozen Mask

A Collection of Poems on Living with Parkinson's Disease

by Denis Murphy

The Frozen Mask

By Denis Murphy

First Edition

Author: Denis Murphy
With additional Poetry and Commentary contributed by Emer Cloherty
Editor: Paul Gilliland
Formatting: Southern Arizona Press
Cover Art: Pixabay – Andrew Martin, UK
All Photographs: Denis Murphy

Published by Southern Arizona Press
Sierra Vista, Arizona 85635
www.SouthernArizonaPress.com

ISBN: 978-1-960038-18-0

Poetry

Dedication

To all those who are living with pain and illness every day. To those who face every day with hope and courage. To friends, family, carers, spouses, and partners - the Real Heroes. Life would be much more difficult without their support, care, and love . To my parents, Benita and Denis, I hope that I have made you proud. And of course, my wife Emer, my rock and my heart.

Foreword

The title of the book *The Frozen Mask* refers to the "Freezing Gait," also known as Akinesia. The mask is explained on Page 13.

I have written this collection of poems to help express my emotions and feelings and to help readers to understand the challenges one faces when living with a degenerative disease. Not only the physical symptoms but the mental difficulties and the impact on one's self-confidence, self-esteem and the erosion of independence and freedom, we take for granted until lost. But also, the life changing challenges that inspire hope and a better appreciation for all life, in particular those close to us.

For more information and other poems, please visit:

Website: https://denismurphy.blog/
Facebook page: Denis Murphy's Poetry

Contents

A Collection of Poems on Living with Parkinson's Disease

Poems by Emer Cloherty

The Rantings and Ravings of a Mad Cork Man!

A Short Story

A Layman's Guide to Parkinson's Disease

Parkinson's Disease and Self-Expression

A good start in life is always a great help and I was lucky to have been born in such a beautiful place. Cork is a city of steps and steeples, of proud tradition and friendly people. Traditional yet progressive, Corkonians are friendly and open minded, confident, and proud, with an awareness of our own unique identity and place in the world. Some of us would be as bold as to suggest that we are the Centre of the Universe! But of course, being a very modest people, we tend not to be too arrogant in our views and opinions. Being generous and welcoming, we love to share our ideas and opinions with the rest of the world, so in keeping with this tradition, I would like, in all modesty, to share these poems and insights with you and thank you in advance for your time and patience.

My name is Denis Murphy and I live in a little village called Riverstown in County Sligo. I was born and reared in Cork city where I grew up in the 60's and 70's. I was always shy and introverted by nature, preferring the world of books and my vivid imagination to the real world. At school I loved history and geography, but I also enjoyed English literature, especially short stories and prose. But poetry for the life of me, I could not grow to either like or appreciate. My mind seemed to switch off and my imagination would wander once Shakespeare or Milton made their appearance in class. Even today, I rarely read poetry. All the more reason I am astounded that it is through poetry I have found a way to express my feelings, emotions, fears, and hopes.

A major turning point in my life came in 2007 when, at the age of 48, I was diagnosed with early stages of Parkinson's Disease (PD). As anyone who suffers from PD, or has a family member who does, will know and understand that it brings about drastic changes, both physically and mentally. It can be very difficult for people with PD to express their emotions, feelings, and to cope with their loss of power and independence.

One of the many physical conditions is called "The MASK." This is when the face muscles become stiff and rigid and expressionless. The eyes appear to lose their sparkle and the mouth seems to be permanently in a "sad" position To the outside world this appears as if the person with Parkinson's Disease (PWPD) is uninterested, bored, and apathetic. But behind this stern facade lies a sea of feelings and emotions.

Another symptom of PD is a problem with vocal expression. The voice becomes weak, and we lose our strength and with this we begin to lose confidence in ourselves. We find it more difficult to express our opinions and ideas in public as we struggle to be heard. So, between difficulties with facial and vocal expression we can withdraw into ourselves and stifle our emotions. All the more need for an outlet to express these emotions, feelings, and fears. So many PWPD find this through art, be it painting, crafts, or writing.

While PD severely restricts our physical and mental activities, there is one advantage. Whether it is the disease itself or the side effects of the medication, it seems to stimulate the creative areas of the mind. So, it is only in the last few years I have begun to compose and express my feelings through my poetry. I have written over two hundred poems to date, not all on PD of course! I write about nature, social issues, mythology, history, philosophy, life, and death.

PD has made a huge difference to my life, not only in health matters. It has made a profound difference in my attitude, relationships, and my whole approach to life. I no longer take things for granted. Even the loss of the simplest things like driving, going for a long walk alone, a trip to the cinema or a concert, or a social event with too many people. Even just being able to run down to the local shop or takeaway. All those little things we don't miss until it is too late. But every cloud has a silver lining; there are some advantages. I can sit back, think about, and observe the world around me and how I relate to people, places, and situations. It has taught me how to appreciate life's gifts and the people in my life. I try to live in the present and make the most of the moment, that is not to say, I don't think about the past, have regrets, or worry about the future. That is only normal, but I do try my best to be as positive as possible, even on some dark days when all I want to curl up and stay in bed.

I have found an inner strength and determination to do the best that I can in any given moment. Without seeking anyone's approval or permission to express myself. I have become more "selfish" and "self centred" but not in the negative sense. I have learned over the past few years or so that if you try to fit in with the world and people and their schedule, you are on a hiding to nothing. The most important person in your life is you! The world must revolve around you!! That is one of the hardest and most important lessons I have learned.

The second, is that I not only have a responsibility to myself but to others. Through my poetry I have found a new medium not only to express myself but to help others to come to a better understanding. We get so caught up in our own little worlds that we forget that we are not the only ones affected by this disease. Our friends, families, spouses, and loved ones are also suffering. At times they can only stand by and watch, feeling helpless and powerless. I am a very lucky man to have such an understanding wife. She has had M.S. for over forty years. So, she has great patience, empathy, and understanding through her own experiences. Without her support, encouragement, and love, my life would be an awful lot darker.

So it is vital that we reach out to them and that is where my poetry is so important as a medium for communication and information and not just a means of self-expression. I feel that the ever-changing challenges have made me look deep inside and I have found a hidden strength I never knew I had. It has forced me to step outside of myself and to observe my lifestyle and how I relate and react to other people and events. I have found the time to sit, think, observe, evaluate, and to see beyond the mist of confusion and distractions of everyday life (or the rat race).

Also, not to accept and get caught up in other people's agendas and conditioning or beliefs but to seek my own path and value my own opinion . I have learned to become self centred and selfish not in the negative sense but in putting ME first at the centre like the eye of the storm, anchored and strong. So, despite having a crippling, degenerating disease, I try to look at the positive things I have discovered or uncovered about myself. And one of these is my poetry.

Parkinson's Disease –
The Day That Changed My Life

I was diagnosed with Parkinson's Disease on the 15th of August 2007. It is hard to believe that it was that many years ago. Looking back, now I know I had some of the symptoms much earlier in my life. Some days it seems so long ago, a different life, a different person. Other days it seems only like yesterday.

I sat across the desk from the man with cold lifeless eyes. His face blank and emotionless, a mask of detachment. I suppose he was used to conveying bad news and had for years trained himself to become emotionally detached and devoid of sympathy or empathy But I'm sure I caught a brief flash of humanity in those pale eyes. In a flat emotionless voice, his words echoed in my head.

"You have early stages of Parkinson's Disease"

I kept repeating the phrase. Sure, Parkinson's is an old person's disease? Then my mind dismissed it as if it was a dream and I barely remember what else was said. I left the room more concerned that my parking disc had expired. It's funny how the mind copes with trauma and bad news.

Parkinson's Disease - A Very Personal Disease

PD is a very personal disease. No two people experience it in the same way. Symptoms vary across a broad spectrum. What might be a major problem for one person is not a major issue for another. While most people may be vaguely aware of some of the physical symptoms, tremors, shaking, slow walk, shuffling feet, and bent gait and stooped posture, they do not realise that there are also many nonphysical things like depression, anxiety, hallucinations, apathy, and procrastination, just to mention a few.

Stress is relative. What freaks me out may seem trivial to you and vice versa. But PD or some side effects of the medication may heighten and intensify those worries and cares. Social outings can be fraught with many worries and anxieties. even weeks before the event. Even the thought of going to a restaurant, cinema, pub, or crowded environment can cause upset and concern. Whether it is a combination of the noise levels, lighting, so many distractions, the fear of falling, or freezing in front of a whole load of strangers. In the early years, I was very self-conscious of people staring at me and thinking that I was drunk, yet there often is no basis for those negative feelings. The event passes and is usually a thoroughly successful and enjoyable occasion.

Narrow Halls and Doorways

Spatial Awareness or lack of, is another symptom or part of the condition many PWPD suffer from as they try to live a "normal" life. This causes freezing in narrow spaces like hallways and narrow doorways. It is as if the walls are closing in and the concentration and energy needed to move is drained and diverted to the fear of getting stuck. When this happens in a public place it is even more disabling and then it becomes a vicious circle - until it is broken and we get to move again. Of course, many people are well meaning and often try to help you when you freeze, for example getting in or out of a lift/elevator.

Yet that is the worst thing they can do. What you need is more space and not to be overcrowded. Recently, I was staying in a hotel and when the doors of the lift opened, I was confronted by a group of about 30 elderly Chinese women, who had just checked in and were all trying to get into the lift with their cases and assorted baggage! Naturally, I froze and got stuck in the doorway. It took awhile for some of the women to realise there was a problem, while others were so intent on talking to each other and they almost walked under me! Finally, they became aware of me and then some of them decided to help! Three of them grabbed my arms and tried to support me and pull me in different directions, while others tried to make a clear way through the crowd, almost falling over bags and other ladies! And of course, they spoke very little or no English! I am afraid my Chinese is also nonexistent! Finally, my wife and I managed to convince them that it would be better for all if they just stood back and gave me space. Every time I met a few in the corridor the next day they would all step back and bow with so much concern and respect.

Parkinson's and Poetry

For some reason unknown to science, PD or the medication or combination seems to boost the creative areas of the brain. It is the lack of a chemical called Dopamine which is vital in carrying the signals and impulses between the neurotransmitters in the brain that control movement. Simple movements we take for granted become more difficult and eventually stop. The medication I am on tries to stimulate the dopamine producing cells and replaces levels of dopamine in order to function. Poetry is one of the few advantages set against loss of independence and dignity. Thanks for your comments, appreciation, and encouragement. It is important and very much appreciated.

Depression and Anxiety

I know a lot of people suffer from depression and anxiety whether they have a condition like PD or MS or not. This can be at its worst in the dark of the night while you are in bed trying to get some sleep. In the past there has been a stigma about mental health, (in Ireland they used to describe as - "Ah sure the poor fellow is suffering from his nerves") - which still exists today, but thankfully people are now a bit more open and willing to discuss their feelings and worries. In the past, I've gone through periods myself, before I was ever diagnosed with PD. Thankfully, I've come through that and learned a lot about myself. Of course, I still get depressed and feel down at times but I now accept that it is part of the healing process as the mind and body try to make sense, learn, and cope with life and our interaction with our lives and our disease. Depression gives us the opportunity to deconstruct, repair, rebuild, and heal our lives and we perhaps look at it in a more positive light.

PD Progression

Over the last few weeks my condition has deteriorated very quickly. It has jumped to another level. I am now experiencing a lot more "off" times and more extreme episodes of freezing and dyskinesia. Not to mention the dystonia and fatigue and the increased anxiety and apathy. I have been to see my neurologist and while he has not increased my medication, he has recommended that I take them more often in smaller doses. This new regime is proving a bit more difficult and trying to fit in mealtimes as protein interferes with Sinemet. The other day while I was walking Oscar, I got "stuck" coming through the village. Two neighbours had to come to my aid, one to take Oscar and the other to help me with my balance. Getting out of the house every day walking my best pal is very important, not just for exercise but to get out and meet people and to be independent. I will now have to consider getting a dog walker and just take shorter walks myself. I am getting very frustrated and angry with this.

A Strange Feeling

I'm not sure if any of you have ever felt or thought about this. But, I'll mention it anyway as it will be of some benefit to PWPD and give their careers an insight into the mixed emotions we experience. I've been feeling a strange mood over the last few days. A sort of sadness, an emptiness, a sense of loss, almost grief. I lost my mother a few months ago but it was not that, or at least not the main reason. Then this morning it struck me like a bolt of lightning. We live in a remote area but both my wife and I do not drive. I have PD so I gave up driving about five years ago and my wife has MS.

One of the main difficulties we were having was with public transport (or lack of frequent and suitable transport) and access to shopping and social events. Things people would normally take for granted. A simple excursion to the beach or local woods. A shopping day out or even just being able to sit in the car and drive, giving us a sense of freedom and independence.
So, a few months ago we bought a car, a big financial commitment considering our income is limited as we are both on disability allowance. We had a driver arranged having paid for her insurance, motor tax etc. However, that didn't work out...and that's another story.

We then decided that my wife would take up the gauntlet and go back on the road. She hadn't driven for twenty years and had to start the whole process again like a raw beginner, provisional licence, mandatory lessons, and tests. She is doing very well and I'm very proud and happy that she has taken to task with such enthusiasm and determination. So why am I feeling this strange emotion ? Then it struck me. I would love to be able to sit in our car and drive anywhere, but I can't. It has reinforced my feelings of lack of freedom and my dependence on other people. Something I had thought I had come to terms with a few years ago.

I know this is just a temporary feeling and now that I've identified and expressed it, it will dissolve and disappear. It's not that I'm jealous or envious of my wife. I'm delighted for her and for the benefit it will bring both of us and enrich our lives and give us back a sense of independence and some normality. So it is a strange mixture of emotions, feeling happy yet sad. I suppose it is a type of grief and a sense of loss of a former life when everyday things like driving and walking were just taken for granted and not fully appreciated until lost to us. That is the reality of PD. It is an insidious disease that slowly creeps up on you. Preventing you from doing things you once took for granted until one day you suddenly realise – "I can't do that anymore." With that comes a feeling of loss of power and control in your life.

They say that in dreams, a car represents your life and if you're behind the steering wheel in the driver's seat you are in control. If you're in the passenger or back seat, then you're allowing someone or something else to drive your life. That may or may not be true, but like everything else in life we take so much for granted and only miss when gone. I suppose that is one of the big lessons we must learn. Appreciate and be grateful for what you have, what you can do and with whom, be they family or friends. Meanwhile I'm going for a little drive, now where did she hide the car keys!

Only joking!

Slaínte

I had to pinch myself this morning. Did my wife really suggest this or was it a hallucination? Yesterday was so warm, I sat outside in the front garden and after lunch, I had a pint of my favourite brew - a pint of Murphy's stout. I wouldn't normally drink alcohol during the day, but I was feeling thirsty and the copious glasses of water did not seem to be slating my thirst. But it being a Sunday and a Bank holiday weekend sure why not?

Afterwards, we went for a drive and had a lovely visit to Glencar and it's beautiful lake and waterfall. I walked up steep slopes and inclines to the waterfall and really pushed the pace. It was a great sense of achievement and satisfaction. I froze a few times on the way down as other people, dogs, and a few running children ran across my path. But I used my techniques and got going again. I am also getting a lot braver and not as self-conscious of wearing the pump with its tube sticking out of my shirt in public. Especially when young kids stop and stare with their mouths wide open.(I just growl at the little feckers or sometimes, I smile at them - it has the same effect - they run ! - One of life's few little pleasures left - frightening young children!)

Later in the evening and night, my energy levels were still high and I was quite lively. My wife remarked on it and asked me what I had done differently - I joked that it must have been the pint! She thought about that for a few seconds, then said it could be the slow release of protein in the stout and might be worth experimenting for a few days., as in having a pint with my lunch every day for the next week! I suppose we do have to make some sacrifices in the name of scientific research. So, I will continue with the experiment today before I wake up and find that this was all a tantalising dream. I shall keep you informed ... meanwhile - is it lunchtime yet?

An Update On Slainte

I'm afraid the experiment did not last very long! Hard to believe but I found the fact that I had the opportunity to drink a pint at lunchtime every day too difficult! If I had been forbidden to drink a pint, I probably would have been able to do so! But alcohol does interfere with medication in general, so where possible avoid mixing both.

Parkinson's Disease and Conversation

As I explained in one of my previous pages, some of the physical effects of PD are tightening of the facial muscles (called the Mask) and the throat area. The voice has become weak and in attempting to hold a conversation, the throat becomes strained and then the muscles often go into spasm, causing the PWPD to choke. There is nothing more frustrating than when this happens, the other person asks, in all earnesty - "Are you OK?" - as if you don't have enough to contend with trying to struggle to breathe as well as expected to answer a question! So, conversation can be difficult or short, which of course is very frustrating for all involved.

Communication and self-expression are vital to humans. Naturally this affects the confidence of the PWPD. So social gatherings can seem daunting. Noise levels and volume can also be very distracting. Hearing conflicting noises and conversations from different directions also causes confusion and stress. So again the result is the PWPD tends to withdraw into him/herself and detach themselves from the conversation taking place either in a group or an individual basis.

It is very difficult to understand or to explain...think of it as if the PWPD is in an *altered state.* Quite happy to be in their own safe, comfortable space, then someone asks a question ... t is like an invasion of someone else's thoughts ... and suddenly you are expected to engage and to respond ... but you haven't been paying attention, you have been off with the fairies somewhere, so you've missed the question. Then you are suddenly aware that you are expected to answer and a bit of panic sets in. There is a *Time difference* between your world and their world, so the response can take a little bit of time to formulate and be reprocessed and translated into coherent speech.

As you may be aware, PD is a result of lack of dopamine and the inability to manufacture this chemical and as a result, brain cells die. Because of the chemical imbalances in the brain, chronic fatigue and exhaustion occurs quite frequently during the day. Yet it can be impossible to sleep ... external noise, cramping muscles, difficulty in being able to lie quietly, and darts of pain like electric shocks. This happens both at day and night. Sometimes the PWPD gets as little as 4 hours of sleep in a 24-hour period. As a result , sleep deprivation, the mind goes into a dream like state and we can operate in this altered state quite well ... then someone asks us a question. So if the PWPD seems to be slow to respond or communicate smoothly, perhaps this may go a little way to explain why..

Duodopa Pump

So, it has been five years since I had surgery to have the tube inserted for my Duodopa Pump. It has been a tough year for my wife Emer and me as we struggle at times to come to terms with my illness and the gradual deterioration in my health and well being. The Duodopa pump itself has taken quite some time to settle and to finally work and be of use in my daily battle against a merciless and cruel enemy. There were days and weeks I really felt so frustrated with the lack of improvement and progress. An immense disappointment and even despair. I remember sitting at the side of my bed and at one point I felt like ripping it out or ringing the Duodopa nurse to ask about the procedure to have it removed and go back on the oral medication. Perhaps our expectations had been pitched too high. But eventually after many trials and errors - we have hit upon the correct dosage and balance for now - this obviously changes as the disease changes and deteriorates again. But we will just have to pay careful attention and keep adjusting.

The main difference between taking the oral medication and the pump method is that I find that the ON periods are very good but the OFF periods are worse. Whereas before I would have a warning that my body was getting tired and fatigue was about to hit, now there is little or no warning ... so I can get tired very quickly, even falling asleep in the armchair or car. But having said that ... the ON periods are better and once I am moving fairly freely I am so happy - there is nothing like the feeling of joy and sense of achievement having walked the promenade at Strandhill or the beach at Dunmoran ... things most people take for granted. The main advantage is that meals can now be taken more or less any time I want. Whereas with the oral tablets, protein was the problem if taken too close to tablets. So, this alone has freed up a lot of time in the day for me.

A Day in the Life ... Morning Ritual

When I wake in the morning, I take the cartridge from the little fridge next to my bed. Depending on how early or late it is, I'll connect the pump and then go back to sleep or just relax for a while. Sometimes I fall into a deep sleep. It takes at least 40 minutes for the Duodopa to hit the system and I usually get an attack of Dyskinesia about ten minutes before it clicks in. Only then can I get out of bed, get dressed and go to the bathroom. Then, I make my way slowly downstairs, feed the cat and dog and slowly come awake, have my breakfast, and catch up on my emails and Facebook. So, I'm never ON in the morning until I've gone through this procedure.

I take one slow release Sinemet as I go to bed. This gives me just that little boost to take me through the night and get moving for the first time in the morning. During the night / early morning I have to go to the bathroom a few times. This can be a real struggle to get out of bed and walk to and from the bathroom. But I move slowly keeping my balance as best as I can. Not easy when you're bursting!

Physiotherapy

I must also give thanks to my two Physiotherapists. Donna and James who have done a wonderful job in helping me with a lot of the physical problems like Akinesia (freezing or the inability to start a movement) and Bradykinesia(slowness). Not to mention the Dyskinesia - the swaying and uncontrollable movement of the body and the Dystonia (painful muscles and cramps).Their enthusiasm and dedication and above all their willingness to LISTEN and adapt exercises and techniques to my needs is very rewarding and satisfactory. I must also mention Caroline McLoughlin, Chairperson of the Mayo branch of The Parkinson's Association of Ireland and her sister Jaqui McCormack for their tremendous support and organisational skills.

So overall, I am feeling a lot more positive about the new year than I was a few months ago. The problem has not gone away nor is it going to, but gradually, as I have come to accept my own limitations and reality, I have come to accept that I now just have to take every day with its own challenges ... and do my best. No two days are the same. My growing dependence on my wife and loss of independence gets me down and angry at times, but life is a series of challenges we must meet and defeat in order to grow and learn. After all, life is a one-way journey and none of us is getting out alive!

Collected Poems on Parkinson's Disease and Self Express

Words and Memories

These are just words that come into my head
Sometimes when I'm walking or just lying in bed
Like unexpected visitors, so strong and intense
As my logical mind struggles to make sense
Concepts and phrases, they come and they go
On the tide of memories, with the ebb and flo

Snatches of memories tantalise and tease
Like whispers and echoes of music on the breeze
Phantoms in the shadows memories so old
Of long forgotten dreams and stories untold
Like ghosts in the mist they struggle to break free
From dungeons so deep, they call to me

Chaos and order, the logical mind
Seeks to understand and solutions to find
But the soul already knows and tries to share
Gently guiding and teaching with patience and care
Through words and visions and whispers in our dreams
But the Ego rarely listens, too busy it seems

A Parkinson's Story

The moment of diagnosis is so surreal
There's been a mistake, this can't be real
Leaving you shell shocked, without any feeling
Your head is numb, your mind is reeling

But it's an old man's disease, you exclaim!
Like that old guy, oh what's his name?
Clutching at straws, your mind in denial
They must have someone else's file

Why is this happening to me?
It's so unfair, how can this be?
What did I do to deserve this fate?
It's all a big mistake, just you wait

But the cold hard truth cannot be denied
The cold harsh feeling deep inside
That feeling of helplessness, the loss of independence
The slow erosion of self- esteem and confidence

While this cross is yours to bear
There is support out there
Reach out to your friends, your family
Be as honest and open as you can be

It is OK to cry, shout and feel angry
To feel helpless and hopeless, lost, and lonely
Acknowledge that you are fragile and tender
Acceptance is not surrender

Parkinson's is progressive and will get worse
Changing my life daily, both a blessing and a curse
But while I have the strength, I will not forget
To cherish every moment without regret.

Do not fear the future, it is not here
For it may be very different from what you fear
Let your regrets and worries fade away
Just be the best you can be today...

A Life in Slow Motion

Another day, another dawn
I stretch my weary muscles and yawn
Another restless night of tossing and turning
Of stupid thoughts and needless worrying
Of aches and pains and cramping feet
I open my eyes, the new day to greet
From shallow sleep and broken dreams
My life has utterly changed, or so it seems

Reality for me now is life in slow motion
Twisting and stretching the fabric of emotion
Between sadness and joy, hopes and tears
Extreme fatigue and anxious fears
On days like these I wonder why
As I try to smile and not to cry
What did I do to deserve this curse
Yet we must remember there are many much worse

A few moments of self-pity, that is allowed
As I struggle to banish this dark grey cloud
Of sadness and anger, of loss and despair
Why me, what did I do, it's just not fair
While I struggle to deal with the simplest task
I remember the man behind the mask
The man I used to be, in another life
Before this struggle and all this strife

And the days I took so much for granted
In pursuit of so many things I wanted
For material things in a fruitless quest
Arrogant and ignorant, we think we know best
So much we take for granted until it is lost
Snatched away before we can count the cost
We do not appreciate until it's gone
But all around us life goes on

But enough self-pity, that's my quota for today
I can't leave negativity get in the way
Like parasites or vampires, they feed if unchecked
If I leave my mind and thoughts unguarded
So, I think of the good things in my life
My family and friends and especially my wife
I struggle to rise and get out of bed
And sit for a while to clear my head

Then ponder for a while on the day ahead
And change my thoughts to be positive instead
Morning light chases the shadows away
And I rise to face the challenges of another day
With courage and determination and mixed emotion
Reality for me now IS life in slow motion.
And be thankful and grateful for another chance
For the precious gift of life and even this slow dance.

Denis Murphy

The Man, the Mirror, and the Mask

The man in the mirror stares back at me
Eyes full of pain and self-pity
Face as tight and taut as a mask
Oh, such effort, even the smallest task
Muscles so heavy with aches and pain
So much effort, so little gain

The man in the mirror stares back at me
Eyes once full of wonder now just apathy
Inside my head that silent scream
Of the little child in a frightening dream
In the dark of the night in a troubled bed
We feed our minds with fear and dread

The man in the mirror stares back at me
Eyes still twinkle full of light and glee
That little child's hopes and dreams still so bright
From deep within a little spark of light
Awakens the adult from its slumber and sleep
And reminds us not to weep

For the things we've lost and left behind
A gentle reminder to be gentle and kind
To that little child who still lives inside
And to the adult we thought had died
The man in the mirror smiles back at me
Eyes full of life and love for me.

A Parky in the Pub

I'll head down to the pub for a drink and the craíc
Sure, I'll be dead long enough on the flat of my back
So, I make my way down to my local bar
On the other side of town for a chat and a jar
Some sit alone, some sit together
Talk of the match or of the weather
And after a pint or two
I need to visit the loo
So, I shuffle and stagger around tables and chairs
Aware of the glances, the pity and stares
Through the noise and the clatter
The gossip and the chatter
I make my way back to my friends and my table
Slow progress but thank God I'm still able
The lads at the bar exchange advice and opinions
To the world's problems and all their solutions
While the girls at the table share secrets and giggle
And walk pass the lads with a sway and a wiggle
The winking and nudging, the secret half glances
Some of the lads even fancy their chances
The smutty jokes and clinking glasses
The lad's loud laughter like braying asses
As they drown out the music like crows in the nest
It's time to go home for some peace and some rest
So, I say my goodbyes in words and mumbles
And make my way home in staggers and stumbles.
The journey home seems twice as long
But I'm on the right road not gone wrong
Two steps forward one step to the side
Steady as she goes watch that stride
Left foot right foot no downward glance
Sure, I might yet get to star in River Dance.

The Man With the Haunted Stare

In a hospital ward between Purgatory and Hell
Trapped in his body, like a prisoner in a cell
Those haunted eyes in a frozen face
His mind and body in a different place
The man in the bed across from me
Laid bare and stripped of all dignity
A mask which hides such fears and terrors
Body wracked with seizures and tremors
His mind still active but cannot share
The man with the haunted stare

By day, they put him in a chair
They wash his face and comb his hair
Fresh and clean from head to toe
All dressed up and nowhere to go
Like a rag doll, battered and broken
Lips move but no words are spoken
Fed by a stranger's hand, he cannot swallow
Those haunted eyes still flicker and follow
Movement and light he is still aware
But he can only sit and stare

Tubes and wires, tablets and pill
Get well card on the windowsill
Family all gather around his bedside
Their pain and sorrow they try to hide
Their eyes avoid each other's gaze
Trying to communicate through the haze
To touch his soul and understand
They gently hold and squeeze his hand
And softly whisper in his ear
But he can only sit and stare

Death stalks these lonely corridors tonight
Come to gather more souls to the light
But not for the man with the eyes that stare
Muscles clenched tightly, eyes filled with fear
His time has not come, he has to wait
He must linger a little longer, such is his fate
Caught between Death and this living Hell
He stares out from his prison cell
To view the world from his bedside chair
The man with the haunted stare.

A Meditation on Constipation

The doctor and nurses ask me the same old question
With my bowels they seem to have an obsession
I'm drinking water with great gusto and passion
Devouring laxatives as if they're going out of fashion
Then back to the loo and resume my mission
To meditate in my seated position
Causing so much inconvenience
It really is trying my patience
Though I try and try with all my might
All through the day and throughout the night
Wasting time, I could be asleep
It so frustrating it makes me weep
I just can't seem to get it right
As I try my best to have a sh*t*e

Like the old song we used to sing
Just don't sit there, do something
About that mean old Scotsman, broken hearted
Who paid his penny but only farted
Bet he was a gas man too
Sitting there for hours on the loo
In the middle of the night all alone
Like a court jester upon the royal throne
Sitting here in such concentration
Causing me so much grief and consternation
Sitting there in anticipation
Just me and my constipation
Belly is so bloated and full of gas
But I just can't get it past my ass

Stomach rumbles and growls like thunder
As I sit there and begin to wonder
Will I ever have a decent crap
Suddenly, I'm a happy chap
Oh, what a feeling of relief
But my joy is short and brief
Flushed with the joy of success
Now I'd better clean this mess.
The rest of the day I'll be on the run
I guess today won't be so much fun
Spending my day on the can
But all that said, I'm a happy man
Filled with satisfaction and delight
Now that I'm no longer full of shite!

Darkness and Shadow

Through darkness and shadow we make our way
Through life's epic journey by night and by day
With a flickering candle to guide and show us the way
Night gathers around us and turns away from the day

But as darkness encroaches like a shroud on the dead
Our fears grow stronger and fill us with dread
Anxiety like a demon gnaws at the soul
Our thoughts turn darker, as black as coal

In the dark of the night the cold fingers of fear
Suffocate our dreams, changing hope to despair
Strangling our dreams in an icy grip
But from the chalice of courage, we take a deep sip

And drive away the ghosts that we most fear
We banish and exile the dark demons of despair
The Ego plays it's tricks like a jester at play
But a glimmer of light and night turns to day

And we cling to that candle, that flicker of light
To show us the path we thought lost in the night
And slowly but surely our feet find the ground
Encouraging and promising a solution will be found

Darkness and light a two-sided coin
Our hopes and our joys together we join
The passing of time, the spring and the fall
The winter and summer, the balance of it all

The ebb and the flow, the tide always turns
And every glorious dawn our fire within burns
A fresh start, our slate is wiped clean
From darkness to light, every shade in between

For that is life, a journey of wonder to explore
And experience and learn and live and adore
The jester still juggles the good and the bad
But we decide our journey, the joyful or the sad.

The Man Behind the Mask

How are you today? People often ask
If they could only truly see behind this frozen mask
Where do I begin to tell you how I really feel
Is it all inside my head or is it really real
How could you understand, how do I explain
My weary bones, my aches, my pain
How long do you have and will you really hear
Will my words cause discomfort or even a little fear
Will you really listen to all my moans and groans
In a voice that whispers in flat monotones
A frozen face hides a turmoil of emotions
As many and varied as the deepest oceans
From high to low and every extreme
And every thought and emotion in between
Like an old man at the end of the day
I shuffle and shake as I make my way
As I struggle to do the simplest thing
To tell a story or a song to sing
Our health and strength we do not appreciate
Until stolen from us, it is too late.
What painful aches and worries we carry
But enough self-pity and thoughts of me
Take off your mask and to me reveal
Tell me how you really feel.
With me you do not have to pretend
How are you today my friend?

Footsteps

Footsteps crunch gravel, shattering my sleep
As I struggle to wake from a slumber so deep
What day is today, is it early or is it late
The postman whistles cheerfully as he opens the gate
The harsh sound of voices as he calls out a greeting
To the neighbour on her doorstep who has been patiently
   waiting
The usual comments about today's weather
As I struggle to gather, my scattered thoughts together

Footsteps sound louder as he comes to our door
The letter box rattles, the post hits the floor
The dog barks loudly, letting us know he's on duty
He takes his job very seriously, our protection and security
Protecting his family, his home and all that
Warning of strangers and that ginger tom cat
The gate slams shut, the hinges in protest scream
Is this real, an illusion, or all just a dream

Slowly I become aware of a dull pain or ache
My muscles groan in protest as they struggle to wake
As I wait for my body and mind to become one
Taking a long time to move is not so much fun
Each day it gets harder and takes longer to rise
I yawn as I stretch and open my eyes
And brush the cobwebs of the night away
Then I fall out of bed to greet the new day

As I button my shirt my fingers start to fumble
On shaky feet I stagger and stumble
Some days it's a struggle just to keep my balance
As I shuffle and shake like a puppet at dance
Between dystonia and dyskinesia, it can really be tough
Energy for simple tasks I never seem to have enough
But life is about adapting and coping every day
And hope that the postman brought some good news today

Keep Your Friends Close
and Your Enemies Closer

The enemy attacks, a silent beginning
It hides for a while until it is sure it is winning
Unseen and unheard, staying out of the light
Slowly and silently, like a thief in the night

Insidious and clever is its nature and style
Invading our body, it tricks us for awhile
Pretending to be a friend, it soon betrays
Slowly revealing, its devious ways

A little twitch, a tremble, a little dart of pain
Is this really happening or am I going insane
Something is not quite right but we dismiss from the mind
It's just our imagination, an illusion of some kind

But our defences have woken and are on the lookout
In the back of the mind there is a gnawing doubt
So, we visit the doctor, we no longer can hide
And to our horror we discover the enemy inside

So, it begins a war between illness and body
While you fret and you stress with growing anxiety
The civil war within exhausts our bodies and minds
Our spirits, our strength and energy it undermines

So how do we cope, what plan, what strategy?
Do we waste all our time caught up in the tragedy
Do we fight it full on and deplete all our energy
Or accept it as a "friend" but who is also our enemy?

Keep your friends close and your enemies closer
Though the gathering storm grows ever stronger
We may bend, we may bow but we do not break
Like a leaf on the breeze our courage we take

Be as gentle and as powerful as water and tide
As we call on the fire from deep inside
With conviction as firm as the earth beneath our feet
We do not bow down, we will not know defeat

Even on days when life seem so dire
Because deep within, there still burns the fire
A glowing ember of hope and your power
Nourish and encourage it like a precious flower

Fix the anchor to that strength within
And let the dance with chaos begin.

Chasing Memories

A memory awakes like a glowing ember
As the mind tries so hard to remember
A flicker of memory buried so deep
Oh, what secrets the soul does keep
Transient thoughts that tantalise and tease
Memories of sadness and some that please
They hint and whisper of a forgotten past
Fleeting, intangible and moving so fast

From a distant time, a different place
The image of a long-forgotten face
Eyes that dance and sparkle like wine
Skin as smooth as silk so fine
Lips that glisten and dare to be kissed
All but forgotten and shrouded in mist
Words of truth left unspoken
A heart left wounded and heart broken

The old man lies there in his bed
Chasing thoughts around his head
A glimmer of recognition in those eyes so green
The ghost of a memory can just be seen
Shadows and sunlight play on the wall
As he tries to remember and recall
But every day it ends the same
He still cannot recall her name.

She came for him, one cold winter's night
Standing by his bed in soft moonlight
She smiled and kissed his brow so tenderly
And whispered in a loving voice so softly
Take my hand, come dance with me
And remember how we used to be
Those sparkling eyes, awaken his mind
A face so graceful, beautiful, and kind

He remembers the first time he saw her fac
And how she made his heartbeat race
Those halcyon days when they first met
Alas so short, but no time for regret
That first shy glance
That first slow dance
That first love's kiss
Those sheer moments of bliss

One more sigh, one more breath
He crosses the line between Life and Death
And waiting there in the welcoming light
She reaches to embrace and hold him tight
As young and beautiful as the day she had to leave
Leaving him heartbroken and all alone to grieve
But their love remains forever and the same
Taking her hand, he whispers her name...

It Could Be You....

Remember the next time you laugh or take the piss
Stop and think and remember this
That stumbling old man may be seriously ill
Resting in that doorway or on that windowsill

Those shaking limbs or trembling hand
Slurred speech, so hard to understand
May not be from drugs or the demon drink
Before you comment on how low can someone sink.

You cannot judge or criticise
The look of pain in those haunted eyes
You do not know his sad story
His long tough journey or history.

Down the street as he lurches and reels
You do not know the pain he feels
The sorrow, the anguish, the phantoms of fear
No one to talk to or to listen or care.

Pause for a moment and think before
You open your mouth like a big barn door
And speak your thoughts out loud
Just to look clever in a crowd

Words once uttered, can rarely be retrieved
And whether true or not, can often be believed.
Do not be so hasty to think as you do
Because someday my friend, it could be you...

A Prayer for the New Day

On a day the world weighs heavily upon your shoulder
When your muscles ache and weary bones grow colder
And the icy cold fingers of despair reach out
To grip your heart and freeze your mind with doubt
And fill your soul with such dread and fear
As you struggle in sadness, not to shed a tear
Afraid that the floodgates may burst open
And sweep you away on a wave of emotion
On a tide of shattered dreams and strangled hope
As you pray for the strength in your struggle to cope
Fearful that you may lose your self-control
And reveal your very fragile and naked soul
On a day when your doubts and fears
Bring you so much sadness and bitter tears

Look to nature for a place to start
Let the breath of life into your weary heart
Look around at so much beauty you can find
And to your heart, be gentle and kind
May the wonders of the world that you see
Encourage you and take you to where you need to be
May you find deep within a tiny spark of light
Let that ember of hope bring you comfort and respite
And ignite a beacon of light so bright
A shield to protect from the dark demons of the night
To comfort and to nourish
To protect and encourage
To guide you to whatever road is right
And wrap you in a cloak of pure love and delight
On your voyage of discovery
On your path and life's journey.

Like a Suffocating Blanket

It clings to me like a parasite
Insidious, it watches by day and by night
Every thought, every move, every waking hour
But I have learned to find my power

From deep inside the fire still burns
Despite all the emotional twists and turns
I feed the flame of resistance and resurrection
With a thirst for knowledge and education

Every day is different from the one before
Each day brings a new challenge knocking on your door
And robs you of something you took for granted
Reinforcing the seeds of doubt already planted

Constant vigilance is required
Though you may be weary and tired
To root out these destructive thoughts you must do
And replace them with both positive and new

In the war against Parkinson's, we must never give in
Though some battles we may lose, others we will win
Some days are hard and some not so bad
To be part of this amazing journey, I am proud and so glad.

Like a suffocating blanket, it clings to me
Will I ever escape and be set free
Perhaps only Death will accomplish that
But I am not yet ready to take that path

I have things to do and people to meet
Songs to sing and friends to greet
I still have lots of people to annoy
To share both my sorrow and my joy

To inflict my poetry on unsuspecting readers
And words of advice to politicians and leaders
Though I have never been to college
I freely share my wisdom and knowledge

Any pearls of wisdom in all sincerity
And all I have learned from Life's University
Without prejudice and in all honesty
Unconditionally and with great modesty.

The Happy Mayo "Cycling" Club

James takes off like a bat out of hell
And says that we're all doing very well
Cycling like a mad man from the county of Mayo
Pedal faster and as hard as you can go
Who ever said "There is no gain without pain" should be
    shot
And that the results will be worth it - I think not !

I'm feeling pain in places I've never had before
I'm sure I'm getting saddle sore
And aches in muscles I never knew I had
I suppose it could be worse, it's not so bad
At least we are indoors from the wind and rain
If we were outside, it really would be a pain

Oh, holy God - I'm dripping in sweat
This training session is the toughest yet
All for the benefit of our health care
Cycling for miles, but never getting anywhere!
I swear this saddle is getting harder and harder
Are we there yet? I can't go much further!

Donna can be quite strict and pushes us more
When we start to flag, she gives a mighty roar
She would have made a great sergeant major
Or in the Gestapo, as an interrogator
Then she flashes that lovely smile
And makes you go that extra mile

Drink plenty water before it's too late
Just make sure you don't dehydrate
My heart rate monitor is going off the scale
And my arse is still as big as a whale
At this rate we'll be ready for the next Olympics or Tour de
    France
A gold medal! We could be in with a chance!

A big Thank You to Donna and James before I go
One hails from Galway, the other from Mayo
Their enthusiasm and passion has to be seen to be believed
By their gentle nature don't be deceived
So professional they will go to any length
Working on your fitness and building up your strength

They listen to your opinion and treat you with respect
With patience and encouragement, you come to expect
For their kindness and compassion, their honesty and care
And Parkinson' Mayo are so lucky to have them here.
Now I'd better finish my exercises or James will start telling
    jokes
And Donna will have to roar again - That's all folks!

The Fool in the School

I never liked poetry when I was at school
The ranting and ravings of some daft old fool
Not for me all those rhythms and rhyme
No thank you , just didn't have the time
Why didn't they just say what they really meant
And not waste my time I could have better spent
Oh, how I hated all that rubbish, that old gibberish
Why didn't they just say it in plain English
No need you see for all this old poetry
Stop beating about the bush or even that tree
Just say what you mean and mean what you say
In plain language please, there's no better way

Generations of misery inflicted on every schoolchild
Keats and Shelley and Byron and Wilde
Milton and Wordsworth and his bloody daffodils
As for that old Shakespeare, just made me sick to the gills
Might as well be looking at the Man in the Moon
Oh, please God let this class be over soon
Why did they have to make it so hard
The craft of the Poet and the art of the Bard
Many years passed and I survived school
But poetry I never needed to use as a tool

Life taught me many lessons, some very hard
While others were a lot better in that regard
I did my very best to keep a balance and check
Then fate dealt me the joker from the bottom of the deck
A disease called Parkinson's has messed with my brain
And because of some medication I take for the pain
I'm now sprouting poetry all night and all day
These words in my head just won't go away
So, I have to write them down before they fade in the fog
From deep within my mind, a memory I did jog
And I smile to myself as I recall those long days in school
The irony of it all, the rantings and ravings of this daft old
    fool!

Denis Murphy

In the Deep Dark of the Bitter Night

In the deep dark of the bitter night
Far from the sanctuary of the new dawn's light
Another sleepless night of worries and dread
From the thoughts running riot Inside your head
You toss and turn but can find no ease
The promise of sleep just torments and tease
The shadows suffocate you in blanket of despair
Your demons gather strength and reappear.

Even your dreams are filled with fears
Ready to betray you and become nightmares
From the thoughts and worries that besiege your brain
Until you find that sacred place to shield you from the pain
To protect and hide from your worries and fears
A sanctuary to shield you from your sorrows and cares
As the ticking clock counts the hours away
Until the light of a brand-new day.

Who Cares for the Carer?

She spends her nights and days
Showing her love in so many ways
That gentle touch
That says so much
In selfless acts and unconditional love
An iron hand in a velvet glove
In a constant battle against the tide
Her worries and fears she tries to hide
The nights are long and often sleepless
Tossing and turning and very restless
Denied the comfort only sleep can bring
Ready for action if his alarm should ring
Sometimes it is so hard to hold back the tears
When she thinks of the future with anxiety and fears
Some days she is too tired to feel
But with courage, determination, and a will of steel
She finds the strength from deep within
Her love for him, will always win
To see beyond this broken shell
The strong young man she knew so well
A man once tall and strong and proud
Stood head and shoulders above the crowd
Now just a shadow of what he used to be
But this she knows, with such certainty
For better or for worse, in sickness and in health
Their love is unbreakable, it is their strength and wealth
His smile is beyond any treasure, worth more than any gold
And their love is more precious as they both grow grey and old.

A Far Away Place

It's 4.30 am and I can't sleep
Not sure if I should laugh or weep
My body is restless and jumping around
Whether I stand or sit no rest can be found
Muscles are cramping and twisted and sore
I'm trying to keep my feet on the floor

Dystonia and dyskinesia battle for my attention
My body and my mind so full of tension
I try to read but my mind won't stay still
Maybe I should take some kind of chill pill
Too tired to move or to exercise
I'll go back to bed, that might be wise

But the world is asleep and oblivious to my pain
Outside the wind blows and here comes the rain
Wrapped in a shroud of shadows so black
Waiting for the light of day to come back
So I lie for a while and contemplate my life
The good things, the bad, the struggle and strife

I take a deep breath and let my mind go
To a faraway place where the wild waters flow
To a place I am safe and have been to before
And find myself on a far distant shore
And there on a beach, I sit on some rocks
And forget about time and watches and clocks

Far removed from the world of mankind
I look around to see what I can find
Waters so tranquil, it can hardly seem true
Away in the distance under skies so blue
A hidden valley can just be seen
And a tall forest so many shades of green

Fragrant and fresh, shining and bright
An aura so clear, a wonderful sight
Cotton clouds and castles in the air
A bridge made of rainbows to get you there
To a magical realm of imagination you will find
A Faraway Place, a sanctuary for the mind

Sights and sounds to gladden my heart
Suddenly I'm back in my bed with a start
I wake to greet morning's first light
A clink in the curtain, so clear and so bright.
A brand-new day brings blessing and new hope
With the strength and the will and the courage to cope.

Denis Murphy

Hospital: A Sick Place

In a hospital ward the daily routine
Your privacy is invaded, as they pull back the screen
What you really need is sleep when you're feeling very ill
They wake you up in the morning to take your sleeping pill

Lying there in an uncomfortable bed
The noise and confusion just wrecks your head
Tearing asunder the healing places of the mind
Peace or tranquility is impossible to find

Blaring televisions and harsh mobile phones
Coughs and splutter, moans and groans
Sniff n snuffle spreading germs and infections
With constant interruptions and intrusions

Visitors from hell, bring their germs and infection
They mean well, but it just adds to the confusion
This is not a place for young children to be
Visitors should be limited and screened very carefully

Then the junior doctors arrive like a flock of geese
All dressed in white, their questions never cease
With their thermometers and stethoscope
Bringing good news and bad, or just a ray of hope

Muscles cramping and painful bed sores
Trolly wheels screech and banging doors
Just another day on the ward of pain
It's enough to drive you completely insane

So just don't sit there by your bedside
Turn the heating down, open those windows wide
And fill your lungs with clean, fresh air
Turn off that TV, so that you can hear

Away in the distance a blackbird calls
A robin answers from beyond these walls
When you are sick and poorly feel
These are sounds to energise and heal.

Mother Nature is here to help and is willing
So, relax and accept the gift of natural healing
Let your body relax and calm your mind
And allow yourself to recover and unwind.

Denis Murphy

Shattered Memories

Shattered remnants of a half-remembered dream
From a different reality, yet so real they seem
Like faded voices on the breeze
Haunted echoes of forgotten memories

Those half forgotten memories
Reach out to grasp and seize
In a vain attempt to have us believe
But serve only to confuse and deceive

Phantoms and illusions of the past
Vague shadows on the wall they cast
Elusive, they flicker and turn and twist
Like illicit lovers longing to be kissed

Whispers in the wind that cry
Gathering secrets as they pass by
Secrets lost as we seek to reveal
Truth or were they ever real?

Listen to both the foolish and the wise
For somewhere in between you will find a compromise
In those fragments of those scattered dreams
Of childish and foolish schemes

Like fallen snow
They come and go
Like fallen leaves, they will fade away
Just as we will too, some day.

We still live in the memories of friends and foe
But our time is short we have to go
And their memories of us will linger on
    But who will remember us, when they too are gone?

Remember When You Used to Dance?

Don't just sit there or you'll vegetate
Get that body moving before it's too late
Though your legs feels like lumps of lead
And you'd rather be tucked up in bed
You have no energy, you've run out of fuel
Take it easy, just relax, stay cool

Watch your step count to three
Don't worry if you're moving slowly
Counting footsteps along the hall
If you need to rest, lean against the wall
Use that mark and step across the line
One step at a time, you're doing just fine

When you freeze and cannot move
Like an old record player stuck in a groove
Or stuck in a doorway or the garden gate
Stand for a moment, then transfer your weight
Take larger steps, watch your balance
Remember when you used to dance

Stand up, sit down, turn around
Lift those feet up off the ground
As high as you can
Well done, good man
Have another drink and take a deep breath
Don't worry, you'll get there yet!

Grasping at Shadows

Come on over here and sit for awhile
It's been some time. I've missed your gentle smile
Tell me all that has happened since I saw you last
And I'll tell you some stories from the distant past

Some days they seem like dreams, not real at all
Like long forgotten memories, too difficult to recall
No matter how hard we try or do or say
Some days, they seem so elusive, so far away

Grasping at shadows, only to be denied
They bob and weave like flotsam upon the tide
And come and go, with the ebb and flo
Were they real or fantasy, impossible to know.

No concept of time and space
No recollection of a name or a face
When the mind wanders, where does it go?
To the place of memories and dreams of long ago.

"Away with the Fairies" - they used to say
Alzheimer's or dementia they call it today
So many people suffer from this disease
Playing tricks with the mind and memories.

Some days are good, some days are bad
Some memories are happy, some are so sad
The present and the past often become entwined
Such are the mysteries and wonders of the mind.

For family and friends, it can be so sad
As they remember you and the good times they had
So make the most of your time, making memories today
Because you never know when they will fade away.

Troubled Times

On the darkest night
You held me tight
From the very start
You held my heart
Through troubled times and raging storm
You kept me calm, safe and warm

A sanctuary for my fragile soul
My sorrow and fears you did console
Gently you held my hand
And helped me to understand
Eased my fears and calmed my mind
With words of comfort, compassion so kind

You lead me through the confusion and the haze
On my darkest hours and darker days
Safe from my sorrows, my worry and pain
Through the darkest nights and dreary rain
You kept my troubled nightmares at bay
Until the light of a brand-new day.

Denis Murphy

The Silent Whisper

Silent Whispers from the caverns of my mind
That elusive memory I struggle to find
Deep in the dungeons , the darkest recesses
As if from another lifetime or someone else's

Silent Whispers in my ear that sigh
Like a beautiful butterfly, fluttering by
Or the faintest touch of a summer breeze
Ghost like, I cannot grasp or seize

The slightest hint of days long forgotten
Whispers of where, whom or when
The past often tinged by needless regret
The future is written, but not yet set

Whether it was a dream or real, I cannot tell
As if concealed by an enchanted spell
Long forgotten in the chaos and confusion
Was it ever real or just an illusion ?

Of Bones and Old Headstones

Do not bury me among the Christian dead
But scatter my ashes to the four winds instead
No priest nor service do I require
Just place my body on the sacred fire

Do not look for me here among the dead
But listen to my voice on the four winds instead
Feel my essence in that gentle breeze
Let your mind be filled with good memories

Remember me in the soft morning light
And later as the shadows of the day becomes night
And in the gentle water that flows by like a dream
Laughing and whispering in that gurgling stream

Feel my presence in the soft morning rain
Far beyond any sorrow or pain
On a misty hill in that sacred place
I am not bound by time and space

Do not sorrow and do not weep
but fond memories of me do keep
gather round, and sing songs of me
let there be laughter, music, and revelry

Do not look for me here in this place of bones
Among forgotten graves and old headstones
For I am not here in this field of tears
I am far beyond any worries or cares

Grieve for a while but do not be sad
Treasure the memories and the times we've had
Remember the joy of you and me
Then let my spirit soar and be free

Denis Murphy

Touched by the Cold Light of Dawn

On the edge of darkness, at the very seams
In the space between consciousness and the world of dreams
Memories awaken and rise to the surface
Of another time and another place
Touched by the cold light of another day
Sparkle for a moment, then fade away
In a place of whispers at the edge of time
A different rhythm, a different rhyme

A heaviness of soul, weighed down by doubt
We struggle so hard to break out
From the prison and chains of a troubled mind
The answers we seek, seem so hard to find
In a woven web of doctrine and rules
Conceived by wise men but enforced by fools
Seduced by the promise of Wisdom's kiss
We grasp at illusions but the moment we miss

Morning light creeps across the bedroom floor
A ray of hope through an open door
A gentle caress to encourage and remind
And chase away the demons of the mind
Peeling away the layers of illusion
Sweeping away the cobwebs of confusion
Stay in the moment and feel the power of now
Yet we fail to grasp this truth somehow

Echoes in the mist, whisper and softly speak
We already know, the answers we seek
Deep inside the ember still glows
What the ego craves, the soul already knows
Though we may search near and far
For Who and What we truly are
Yet we fail to listen to the voice within
Perhaps that is our greatest sin?

Bent, Battered, but Never Broken

I suddenly stir and begin to wake
As my body and mind try to integrate
Bedroom full of shadows and dappled light
Day has chased away the night
As I slowly move this tired body
I've slept for a few hours but still feel weary
But I will not admit defeat
As I struggle to stand and get to my feet
Like an old man I stagger and sway
As I slowly and carefully make my way
Creaking bones on creaking floor
And freeze for a moment by the bedroom door
Some days I feel like I am ninety-three
Trapped in a cage ,struggling to break free
Like a pacing tiger in a gilded cage
Moving so slowly like a man twice my age
Chronic fatigue affects both body and brain
Aching muscles and darting pain
Like electric shocks on aching bone
I wish just for one day they would leave me alone
Some days I just feel like crying
But Inside, I'm still alive and dancing
I am still that child ,that strong young man
So I will continue to do all that I can
Someday I will be just bones and dust
Life goes on as it surely must
Parkinson's has robbed me of a lot
But I can still dream and scheme and plot
I still have things to do and places to be
People to meet and many wonders to see
And still many words left unspoken
I may be bent and battered ,but I will never be broken.

The Winds of Change

As we dance and we weave through the eddies of life
Twirling and swirling, holding on for dear life
To the rocks of insecurity and foundations of sand
To dreams and schemes and plots so grand
To the thoughts and opinions many so dark
Tumbling and fumbling like fools in the park
In a frantic search for the dream so bright
Demented souls seeking the light
Phantoms of illusion, ghosts of greed
In the battle between want and need
But the winds of change blow daily through life
Some strong, some subtle, some cut like a knife
Shaking and shattering our illusions of might
And outdated insecurities we believe to be right
Yet deeply within is the will to survive
To enjoy each day and to feel alive
We have the strength and courage for the challenges we
    must meet
To stand up to and fight, to face and defeat
We can only live our lives day by day
And let the winds of change blow our fears away.

Poems by Emer Cloherty

Look Closer

You might only see the trembling hands,
but I see the steadfast and tender way he holds my heart.
You might only see the stern and unresponsive stare,
but I see the depth of intelligent compassion behind the
    eyes.
You might only see the slow and stumbling, shuffling walk,
but I see the Hero, striding forth to meet the challenge of
    each day.
You might only see the inexorable decline; the inevitable
    losing of independence and dignity,
but I see the gradual development of patience and of deep
    undying love.
You might only see Parkinson's,
But I see my Beloved.

by Emer Cloherty

My Precious Parkie Penguin

My Precious Parkie Penguin
    is proceeding with great patience
        from the bedroom to the bathroom
            in the middle of the night.
Just a journey of five metres
    not a problem for most people
        but for Denny after midnight
          It's a monumental fight.

With the stooping Parkie Posture
    He looks so much like a penguin.
        And his halting shuffling feet
           seem to be stuck onto the floor.
But with quiet strong persistence
    he refuses to surrender
        as he steers around the corner
          and navigates the door.

Like the great Antarctic Emperor
    he struggles, uncomplaining.
        And although to you that battle
           may seem trivial or slight,
it's an epic icy struggle
    of his will against this illness.
        And my gentle husband takes it on
          with true heroic might.

by Emer Cloherty

Because

Because you stumbled,
   I learned to slow my step.
      I learned to see your path.
         I learned to love you more.

Because you became weaker,
   I learned that I am gentle.
      I learned that Love is tender.
         I learned you love me deeply.

And love is what's important,
   not pills or spills or illness,
      or even strength or weakness.
         Just simple, wondrous Love.

Because I love, I care.
   Because I care, I love.
      As time goes on,
         I will not become your carer,
         but your Lover.

by Emer Cloherty

The Disabled Tango

Hallways and doorways,
   Too narrow for two.
      I can't step sideways
         And neither can you.
Nor can we reverse,
   We'll be stuck here all day.
      So, we just do
         The Disabled
            Tango.

M,S. and P.D.
   We, a matched pair are.
      Each one the patient
         And each one the carer.
Dancing and Laughing
   And shuffling our way,
      Just doing
         The Disabled
            Tango.

by Emer Cloherty

When the Sky has Fallen

I don't need to listen to fear,
    the solution is in my own hand.
        And I needn't give in to despair,
            when life has not gone as I'd planned.
I just sift through the wreckage and ruin,
    but don't linger on what I have lost.
        Discarding the broken sharp pieces,
            I let go of the pain and the dross.

Only then, in the ruins I discover,
    among all the scraps left behind,
        seeds for the future and balm for today.
            They are there in my heart and my mind.
I know they are strange and old fashioned,
    these things that can't be bought or sold,
        But when I lost all that the world holds dear,
            I found these were worth more than gold.

Virtues, your mother would call them.
    Weaknesses, some people say.
        But they're powerful tools in the hard times,
            though they can't make the pain go away.
They can lessen the pain by removing
    all the extras that needn't be there.
        And when I have only legitimate pain,
            that is so much more easy to bear.

The biggest unnecessary pain in my life
    was the one that I call "Oh Poor Me",
        and I ditched it by learning to focus my mind
            on what IS not 'what I wish would be'.
And once I accepted the notion that pain
    is quite normal in everyone's life,
        I could not then cry 'this is so unfair';
            although that lesson cost me some strife.

I then had to loose "Kiss it better",
    and 'magic it gone with a pill'.
        There is no magic spell or elixir
            that can save me from every ill.
But there is such a thing as enjoying
    the small treasures and beauties each day.
        The more I am grateful, the more great they
    become,
            till the sorrows they start to outweigh.

Then the spectres of Social Convention;
    Independence, Career, and all that
        tried to say that my life was now worthless.
            So I kicked them into a cocked hat.
I asked 'what's the worst that can happen?'
    They said 'all your money will go,
        and all your prestige will soon vanish'.
        I thought about that, and said 'So?'

I know I can live very simply,
    and I don't need the care and the sorrow
      of trying to do what I cannot do now
        out of fear of being hungry tomorrow.
Tomorrow will have to look out for itself,
    I have plenty to deal with today.
      When I finally learned how to focus on that,
        one more silly fear went away.

I learned Patience and Courage, Compassion and Joy,
    since the day the sky fell on my head.
      I might be just limping and stumbling along,
        but hey Guys, I still ain't dead!

by Emer Cloherty

The Rantings and Ravings of a Mad Cork Man!

A Selection of Poems on Nature, Mythology, Life, and Death

And now for something completely different! The following poems are just a few examples of the various subject matter covered by my poetry, besides Parkinson's Disease and its related conditions. These poems are about nature, mythology, history, current affairs, politics, social commentary, philosophy, life, and death. In fact, just about anything else I have an opinion on or just when I need to have a good rant! I hope to publish more of these type of poems in future volumes. These are just fifteen examples. Enjoy!

And Here be Dragons

A silken cobweb caught in the breeze
Like a satin sail on emerald seas
Or a fairy ship that sails the skies
Above the seagull's lonely cries
Far above the cotton clouds
Far away from human crowds
Moonlight magic and silver cloud
Magic castles float tall and proud
And shapes so wondrous we cannot describe
What magic and wonder these clouds can hide
And far below where dragons sleep
Beneath sacred lakes and oceans deep
The heartbeat of the ocean floor
Like a drum beat upon a distant shore
Where Mermaids sigh and softly weep
Singing sad songs, what secrets they keep
In dreams our spirits soar and fly
Where magical dragons rule the sky
On wings of azure blue and emerald green
And flashes of crimson can just be seen
Through clouds of silver our spirits glide
On dragon's wings we soar and ride
To fantastic places and faraway lands
And endless beaches of golden sands
Remember as a child we had such dreams
When we grow up, we forget it seems
Innocence lost and imagination restrained
Our hopes and dreams in dungeons chained
Time to rediscover our childlike ways
And the wonders of our halcyon days
What wonderful places in our minds we can go
If we just sit and let our spirits flow.

Denis Murphy

Hunter's Moon

A sliver of fiery sunlight streaks
Above the edge of the jagged peaks
Day fades away and quietly dies
Across a canvas of darkening skies
Storm clouds gather overhead
Sullen grey skies, as dark as lead
Our thoughts and prayers are carried away
In the embers of the dying day

A bird chirps sharply, a plaintiff call
The forest pines stand gaunt and tall
Shrouded in shadow and half light
Ghostlike in the evening twilight
Light and darkness embrace and meet
As the shadows wait for day to retreat
Daylight dissipates and fades away
And heralds the end of another day

A full moon rises, a pale fiery glow
Casting her veil on a slumbering world below
Embracing the land in her protective shroud
Her night vigil begins as she dances on cloud
Caressing deep oceans with her silvery light
Dancing on water sparkling and bright
Scattering star light along and the Milky Way
The world in her arms until the break of the day

Seasons come and seasons go
The turn of the tide, the ebb and the flo
The hunter's moon waxes and wanes
In our world, nature still reigns
On these late Autumn nights
The bitter cold wind stings and bites
By the light of the hunter's moon
Winter, will be here soon

The Invisible Man

A crow takes flight with a loud cry
Dark shadows circle against a leaden sky
A bitter cold wind bites both man and beast
From faraway lands in the frozen North-East
A warning of more severe weather on the way
On a grey and sullen, cold winter's day

Huddled and shivering in a dark doorway
A lonely old man now broken and grey
Cold, frozen and chilled to the bone
Crumbled blanket for a bed on cold stone
Torn and damp, no more than a rag
A few precious possessions in a plastic bag

Once a proud man now just a shell
Now just another tragic story to tell
Once a mother's heart filled with pride
Another human being fallen by the wayside
Betrayed and discarded, like an old rubbish pile
Another statistic on a government file

Same old man on a busy street
Hungry and cold, nothing to eat
Almost invisible to the passing crowd
Like a dark shadow in a darker shroud
As if from another world or different space
Just another person without a face

An indifferent world just passes by
Oblivious to his heartbroken and silent cry
Too busy to see the human behind the mask
To stop and look, listen or to ask
They do not know or even see
Before them this Human tragedy

A little child stops and shyly looks up
Then places a coin in the old man's cup
Memories surface of another man's life
He too had a fine home and a loving wife
And a beautiful daughter with golden hair
He bows his head and wipes away a tear

Frowning faces and judgmental eyes
Too busy to hear his silent cries
Some irritated and even annoyed
While others look away and try to avoid
A mixture of fear, embarrassment, and pity
Such is life on the streets of our city

Denis Murphy

A Place of Magic, a Place of Dreams

On a cold winter's morning, such a beautiful day
Down through the town, I made my way
And took the old path by the riverside
And watched for a while, a pair of swans glide
On waters so peaceful, so calm and serene
A balm for the soul, nature's perfect scene
By the old stony bridge I did take a seat
And listened for a while to the soft music beneath
Giggling and gurgling and making its way
Singing it's wild song by night and by day
From the wild places, rivers and streams
A place of magic, a place of dreams
While a lonely sentinel stands on a log
A heron, half hidden in early morning fog
Like an old grey fisherman, patient and still
While far in the distance on a lonely hill
A hungry fox hunts, while the hare hides and waits
Nearby an ancient yew tree guards the gates
To a field where, in silence, stands a circle of stone
The race who built this, their fate unknown
Whispers of druids and priests and magic they tell
Tales of ancient heroes and villains and warriors who fell
In a battle long forgotten
Between the Gods and mortal men
Mystery and magic haunt this place
Time outside time, a sacred space

The present and the past go hand in hand
The ancient stones like a silent witness stand
The circle of stone forms a magical ring
In the sky above, a raven takes wing
A keeper of secrets, a guardian of dreams
In this sacred place, nothing is what it seems
In the half light, shadows take form

And the gods gather before the coming storm
Spirits of water and of the rivers and lakes
Of sacred groves in deep forest glades

In this sacred place, this magical stone ring
The ancient ones gather to pray and to sing
From the hills and the valleys and villages they come
In ceremony and ritual, to the heartbeat of the drum
In this cathedral of stone, the sacred fire burns
While the wheel of time in an endless spiral turn
From birth in the east to death in the west
From order and chaos, a time of unrest
The journey of life we must make
And hard is the road and path we must take
A new day dawns, a crimson sunrise, a bleeding sky
Another day, another season, another year rolls by
In the circle of life and the wheel of time
From the cradle to the grave, the passage of time
A time to laugh and a time to weep
And the stones stand silent, their secrets they keep
In a field of half-light, shadows, and shades
The shadows gather around me, as the vision fades

I suddenly wake as if from a dream
Of battles and heroes, so real it did seem
And find myself back on the bridge by the river
So, I sit for a while, and give a little shiver
As I gather my thoughts and say farewell to the river
Then make my way home just in time for my dinner

Just Another Pawn

A blackbird's song. A plaintiff cry
The Angels weep in a blood red sky
A moment of beauty in this wretched place
A lonely lament for the human race
The Angel of Death visits this day
And many a soul will be carried away
Death stalks like a ravenous beast
And on the dead and the dying feast

Jagged trenches like scars in the land
Barbed wire fences bite foot and hand
Flesh ripped and torn by shrapnel and shell
This place of horror, a living hell
Bullet and bayonet, cold hard steel
Rotting corpses and rutted wheel
Bones shattered and minds broken
What horrors and demons have they awoken?

Horror walks this bloody Battlefield
For so many, their fate has been sealed
A young boy, face down in the mud
Life ebbing away in rivers of blood
An unknown soldier, just another pawn
Some mother's child ,who will never see the dawn
Lost among the screams of terror and agony
Lambs to the slaughter for king and country

Well behind the battle lines
Swilling Brandy and the finest wines
Pompous generals play the game
Their blunders, acceptable losses, all in the name
Behind the smiles they cannot hide
The Pawns they've sacrificed on the fires of pride
As they raise their glasses and sing
For God, for country and for king.

A blackbird's song, a lonely lament
In a field of crosses, headstones, and cement
Just sit for a moment and take your ease
A carpet of poppies sway in the breeze
Each one a memory of a hero who fell
Lest we forget, this place was once hell
For the fallen, the brave, the boys, and men
May their sacrifice never be forgotten.

Ode to Oscar

He is gone now, my faithful friend
I held him close to the very end
He is now beyond any sorrow or pain
My walking companion through sunshine and rain
Through storms and sullen clouds of grey
To blue skies on a midsummer's day
On misty mornings down by the river
In freezing fog that made us shiver
It was precious time, time well spent
As you followed a trail or an exciting scent
Frosty morning, cold blustery days
But now we must go our separate ways

There were days when I left you down
When I had to go alone or into town
But you always greeted me with wagging tail
So happy to see me, without fail
And happy just to share some time
As thick as thieves, we were partners in crime
Barking madly at the cat on the wall
Chasing crows and playing ball
Then eating my slippers my newspaper
Running off with and skinning my sliotar
You loved chocolate biscuits and anything sweet
And the odd juicy bone as a special treat
Ready and willing to clean the dinner plates
Neighbourhood watch sitting at the front gates
Always seeking mischief and innocent fun
And a warm welcome for everyone

While we walked through field and wood
Through marsh and meadow, whenever we could
You left your message on every tyre and tree
On every pillar and lamp post you had to wee
And listened patiently to my plans and schemes
My troubles, my worries, my hopes, and my dreams
You are gone now, my faithful friend
Death comes to all in the very end
I will miss your gentle snores and your eyes so bright
With the joy of the moment and simple delight
And the joy that you gave me right to the end
Thank you Oscar, my faithful friend.

Denis Murphy

The Priest

We never really knew the man, we barely knew the priest
They said he came from Wexford or somewhere in the east
He never spoke of his family or of his childhood days
His past he kept to himself, securely locked away

He was patient, compassionate, and always very kind
A scholar and a gentleman, a sharp and brilliant mind
Hurling was his passion and he loved a glass of wine
To the outside world his life appeared normal and fine

He wore a mask of contentment, to hide his bitter pain
Loneliness at times almost drove him insane
The lack of intimacy and another human's touch
There were long and lonely nights when it almost got too
     much

His struggle with self-doubt that felt so very real
His crisis of faith, he could not reveal
Or share with a close friend on how he really felt
Not even to God, at whose altar he knelt

He was on call, every night and every day
And always ready to dash away
His parishioners kept him occupied and busy
Though Friday night's bingo used to drive him crazy

They kept him up to date with the latest news
Invited to every wedding, he could not refuse
At every funeral and christening, he was there
The old ladies doted on him and lavished him with care

That morning he had received a letter
From the bishop on an urgent matter
But his car was contrary, something wasn't right
He decided to take the train and stay overnight

It was a dreadful night of wind and rain
He was rushing to catch the very last train
He had been delayed due to a sick call
When his car went crashing through the wall

The funeral was well attended, there was a massive crowd
There were lots of speeches and kind words said out loud
They spoke of his good deeds and his faults there were so
     few
The man behind the priest, that no one really knew

A stranger came among them, a stranger dressed in black
Standing by the graveyard gates, at the very back
A whisper rippled through the crowd, like a silent wave
A single red rose, she placed upon his grave.

Down to the River Side

When the worries of the world weigh heavily on my mind
A peaceful place, a sanctuary I will find
Down to the river side I will often go
And listen for a while to the wild waters flow
Giggling and laughing and singing its song
No worries or cares as it hurries along
Carefree and joyful, magical, and bright
Dancing and tumbling, in the early morning light
Sparkling like silver and diamonds that glisten
And there for a while, I will sit and just listen

The birds sing a chorus, so beautiful and so clear
A symphony of song in the early morning air
Sweet harmony so natural, such a beautiful sound
In all of our music, none better can be found
While the wind in the trees softly sings along
No human could compose so wonderful a song
And the bees and the insects all join the performance
So beautiful, so natural, such rhythm and balance

So just sit and listen and relax for awhile
To Nature's wonderful gift and let yourself smile
The joy of the moment just there in your hand
The soul and the spirit know what the mind seeks to
    understand
Be both grateful and humble for this wonderful chance
Such a privilege to be part of this Creation Dance
For the gift of life and a brand-new day
And feel all your worries and cares fade away.

A Grumpy Christmas Fairy

Christmas time comes around so fast
In that starring role I am once again cast
They take me out of my box once a year
About my vertigo, they really do not care
And place me on the top of the tree
Where I feel a little sick and rather dizzy
Perched here precariously, at such a lofty height
Grimly holding on, throughout the long night
Surrounded by all that glitters, baubles and balls
Tinsel and Holly, hanging on the walls
Those flashing fairy lights are such a pain
Pretty soon, I'll have such a migraine

Locked in the attic, I'd much rather stay
Throughout the long and weary day
The cat climbs and knocks another bauble or ball
He'll be happy when tree will tumble and fall
And I'll fall down and break my neck
Oh, I do hate Christmas, I'm a nervous wreck
And just to make my day, at the foot of the tree
The dog cocks his leg and does what comes naturally
It really pisses me off, as I hold on tight
Happy Christmas and all that shite
It's not very nice, it is really such a farce
You try having a Happy Christmas, with a tree stuck up your
    arse.

A Fisherman of Words

They come to me like drunken butterflies
That dance and flash before my eyes
Images, imagined and yet so real
I can reach out and almost feel.

A word, a phrase, a half-forgotten line
It may not even be one of mine
Of a half-forgotten dream
Or some long abandoned scheme.

A breath that lingers in the air
That no one else can hear
The faintest whisper in my ears
An echo before it disappears.

Leaving no trace
Of a long-forgotten face
A shimmer on the cosmic surface
Of another time, another place.

Like scattered leaves on the breeze
I struggle to capture and to seize
To gather them, like a kingfisher on the wing
Each one a jewel, a sparkling shiny thing.

And so, I must follow, I have no choice
To let them be heard, I must lend to them my voice
To bring them to life even for a little while
To create a memory, a tear, a smile.

A Fisherman of Words is what I have become
A Catcher of Dreams at the setting of the Sun
A Weaver of Tales under the Moon's soft light
A Dancer of Hope beneath the Stars so bright.

A Blood Moon Rises

A blood moon rises, peering through dark cloud
A cry in the forest, chilling and loud
Like a demon, from another world
Tendrils of clouds, like banners unfurled
Casting twisted shadows in the moonlight
On this cold and dark winter's night.

Deep in the forest on a haunted hill
A raven's cry, sharp and shrill
From the highest towers of the castle keep
To the dungeons below, so dark and deep
Memories trickle down through the years
Ripples of music, laughter, and tears
Echoes of footsteps down ancient hallways
From those distant and long forgotten days

Ghosts and phantoms now abound
Among the briars, nettles, and stony ground
Through ancient arches and broken doorways
Up crumbling and winding stone stairways
Ivy now creeps on crumbling walls
Down dusty corridors and musty halls
Where lords and ladies danced in candlelight
To haunting music, long into the night
In the banquet hall, they gathered for the feast
Regaled by tales of dragons and fearsome beasts

A harpist weaves magic in music and song
Bringing tears to the eyes as they sing along
Some drink to remember while others to forget
Recalling sweet memories and some of regret
Music and laughter and young lovers dreams
And in the darkest corners, hatching plots and schemes
Conspiracies and intrigue, loyalty and betrayals
Now cobwebs shimmer like silken veils
Down dusty corridors where dappled moonlight
Flickers and dances in pools of soft light
Evening falls, as the pale light fades
A twilight world of shadows and shades.

The Shining Ones

The Iron mountain stands mysterious and aloof
With banks of cloud across it's hidden roof
Like ghostly tendrils they seem to reach
Where no mortal eye can breach
As if paying homage to Gods of old
In the myths and the legends that are still told
Of heroes and warriors, battles and blood oaths
Of mysterious and magical flying boats.

Mist captures morning's pale light
Chasing away the shades of night
Through swirling silver mist they appear
Then vanish as quickly into thin air
Shifting shadows between our world and theirs
Ghost like, the Faery Host reappears
Through secret paths they have made their way
An Tuatha Dé Danann has come home to stay.

Standing on the edge of a dream
By the mystical waters of a silver stream
Is She shadow or really there
Her wind tossed flowing silver hair
Like a billowing cloak of silver grey
On the dawning of a brand-new day
On the turning of the celestial tide
The Shining Ones, Danu's people ride.

According to legend, the Tuatha Dé Danann came to Ireland on flying ships, surrounded by dark clouds that engulfed them. It goes on to say that they went on to land on a mountain in County Leitrim now called Sliábh an Iarainn (mountain of the iron).

The Tuatha Dé Danann, the people of the Goddess Danu - the earth- mother goddess. They had come to Ireland from the "islands of the north" and fought the Formorians to rule these lands, before the coming of the Millesians (the Celts). They have also been associated with the fairies or the Shining Ones.

Denis Murphy

The Centre of the Universe

In my dreams, I often go
To where the waters of the river flow
To the place I was born by the river Lee
Of my childhood days and memory
A beautiful city of steps and steeple
Of good humoured and friendly people
Of bridges, churches, cobbles and spires
A place to warm the heart's desires

Shandon bells ring loud and clear
The heartbeat of the city, fills the air
The four faced liar and it's salmon of gold
Looks out on a city both modern and old
Sandstone and limestone, red and white
From Patrick's hill, such a beautiful sight
With winding streets of charm and beauty
And quays softly kissed by the river Lee

No better way to spend a day
Than doing Pana, as the locals say
Patrick's street to the Grand Parade
The Mardyke, the Park and it's leafy shade
Just to stroll along, or stop to talk
The shaky bridge and lovers walk
Down the Marina to the Atlantic pond
To Blackrock castle and the harbour beyond

The English market, such a wonderful place
Thriving and exciting, a vibrant space
A place so famous, even a visit by the queen
And the ugliest fish you've ever seen
Tripe and onions, crubeens and drisheen
And the famous black pudding from Skibbereen*
The smells and sights I recall so clearly
The sound of laughter echoes in my memory

Blackpool girls and the boys of Fairhill
The clash of the ash is still such a thrill
Jack Lynch, Jimmy Barry, and Christy Ring
The many pubs where we used to sing
To drown our sorrows. or celebrate
The Long Valley for a "doorstep full of mate"
Washed down with a pint of Murphy's stout
Or a Beamish or two - it's your shout!

The bells of Shandon ring out
Time for another pint of stout
The Phoenix, Dan Lowrey's and the Hi Bi bar
We would often go, for the craic and a jar
Canty's and the Old Oak down the street
Or in the Lobby bar we would often meet
Where bards and poets weave song and verse
From the Centre of the Universe !

A poem about my beloved Cork city and precious memories of my childhood and teenage years.

*The famous Black pudding is actually from Clonakilty but I couldn't think of anything to rhyme except Guilty or Filthy and I don't think that would have gone down well with the locals - I do want to go back there! So Drisheen/Skibbereen will have to stay.

Happy Birthday Dad. It's Been A While

Happy Birthday Dad, it's been awhile
I miss your frown, your laughter, your smile
I'll just sit for a moment by your grave side
And deal with the emotions I've tried to hide

It's been awhile since we have spoken
My heart still hurts, I'm still heartbroken
Where do I begin, where do I start
Unspoken words straight from the heart

Memories flood back and I try not to cry
As I remember that twinkle, that glint in your eye
And just for a moment your stern mask slips
Revealing the faintest trace of a smile on your lips

I think about the support and advice you gave
Standing here, alone by your grave
The wind turns and it begins to rain
I will never know your sorrow and pain

Or the tough decisions you had to take
And the sacrifices you had to make
In difficult times, you did your best
Now it is time for you to rest

You had played your part and played it well
You had no more to teach or stories to tell
In the book of Life, the final page
It was your time to leave, to exit the stage

In the end, Death comes to all
Neither man nor beast can resist its call
I still feel the sorrow, the emptiness, the pain
But also, your love, standing here in the rain

As I turn to leave, both humble and proud
The sun peeps from behind a dark cloud
A sliver of sunshine falls on your graveside
Just a little twinkle, like the smile you used to hide.

The Long Journey Home

A winter evening, darkness is falling
My thoughts are of home and loved ones calling
At the end of day, journey's end
Eager to see my faithful old friend
As I gather my cloak tightly around me
A bitter North wind bites sharply
Howls and shrieks like some demon from hell
From the old ghost stories my grandfather used tell
Deep in the woods the trees and branches sway
The darkness gathers to banish another day
Opaque light, shadows, and shades
Casting shadows and shapes as daylight fades
Shadows dance, swirl, and sway
Like tortured souls, awaiting Judgement Day
Ghostly forms and grotesque faces
From those dark and frightening places
Tales from nightmares and horrors of long ago
Deep in the mind where no one should go
Where dreams linger, at the edge of reality
There is no difference between the sane and insanity

The Sun sinks behind the edge of a hill
A frozen moment as Time stands still
The dying rays through branch and leaf
Flicker like fireflies, sparkle so brief
Dark silhouettes circle against crimson skies
Shattering the silence with their piercing cries
Raucous ravens return to roost for the night
A pale moon rises, casting soft Moonlight
Silver stream shimmering at my feet
By an old oak tree, I sit beneath
Gnarled and bent and oh, so very old
What Secrets and Memories do these limbs hold?
A Guardian of Secrets and memories untold
Wisdom and Knowledge so Ancient and Old
Sanctuary and Silent, I rest for awhile
And think of my loved one and her warm smile
On my journey home through dark and lonely ways
A bright light awaits and happier days
A warm welcome among family and friends
Home, that is where my journey ends

The Girl with Green Eyes
Short Story

There was always something strange about that child. Even the other children would fall silent as she approached. A curious mixture of awe, reverence and a hint of fear. Huddled in hushed voices they would glance over their shoulders as she approached. Some days she would speak to them but others she would just stand and stare. They would greet her with silence until the tension became too much and one of them would giggle or snort. Suddenly their courage would return and the name calling and mocking would begin. Children can be very cruel. But she would just stare at them as if oblivious to their taunts and insults and walk away.

One day one of the boys, emboldened and encouraged by the girls, ran after her and caught her long ponytail. It was the last time anyone did. He had a bruise on his arm for a long time. They began to suspect she was a witch or even a changeling, one of the Faery Folk.

Even the adults had been heard to whisper their suspicions as they shivered, shrugged their shoulders and blessed themselves on the church steps after Sunday Mass. Perhaps it was her strange and old fashioned clothing or something in the way those green eyes would stare and transfix you. As if she could reach inside you and see into your very soul.

Her mother, God help her, had passed away in childbirth leaving two young children and a grieving husband who could never cope. A strange man to begin with, then the drink took him as he tried his best to cope and not drown in a sea of sorrow and despair. Often, he would just be sitting by the side of the road like a lost soul. The children would try to hurry by before he became aware of them and call them over. Beckoning with his grubby and sweaty hand. Sometimes he would reach out and grab you if you weren't quick enough and hold onto your hand or arm, squeezing until you almost cried out, like a drowning man too desperate to let go. There was terror in those eyes, a tortured and demented soul. And one cold winter's morning, they found him, frozen and still by the side of the road.

The elder sister had become a little mother and was doing the best she could in looking after her younger sibling until her health left her. She later joined a convent.

There were aunts and a few well-meaning neighbours who looked in from time to time. But mainly the family were left to themselves. THAT family as they were called.

Years rolled by, some slowly, some swiftly. The children grew up and the adults grew older, and every passing season brought its own changes and experiences. The young girl blossomed into a beautiful young woman and the local boys took note but still were hesitant to approach or engage with the girl with green eyes. She was still wild and was often seen roaming the countryside by night. Some said she took the form of a wolf and howled at the moon, a lament for her long-lost family. Others said she was a witch and danced with the faery folk

Then one night while on his way home from the pub and none the worse for a few drinks, a young man stumbled and fell by the roadside. Hitting his head, he went out like a light. God knows he could have frozen or bled to death in the early morning snow, but that night God sent an angel to gather him up and bind his wounds.

He woke for a brief moment, confused and disorientated. In the shadow and half-light, he thought he could make out the form of a large wolf at the foot of his bed and found himself staring into the greenest eyes. But somehow, he knew he was safe and protected and fell back into a deep sleep.

And many years passed...

An old couple sitting by the fireside. He turns to his wife and smiles and sees the sparkle in those eyes so green. The windows to a beautiful soul and thanks God for falling by the roadside.

She just smiles.

I swear that some days I still have that bruise on my arm.

A Layman's Guide to Parkinson's Disease
Written by Emer Cloherty
As in life, my wife has to have the last word!
Ouch! I didn't see you there my love...

Here's a layman's guide to Parkinson's Disease, without the medical jargon. Parkinson's disease happens when a little section of brain-cells in the underside of the brain start to die off. These brain-cells have the job of producing a chemical called Dopamine. Dopamine is the chemical needed for messages to move from one nerve cell to another. Messages have to move from one cell to another for any part of the body to do anything. If your hand needs to reach out to something, and then grip that something, and then move that something somewhere else, that is a whole lot of messages that need to move from one cell to another. And if your hand needs to stop moving, that is a whole other lot of messages. Without enough dopamine, the body is no longer getting the right messages in the right order, and things start to go wrong.

Early in the disease only a small number of the dopamine-producing cells have died, so the symptoms are only slight. The first symptom most people notice is called a Tremor. This is when some part of the body develops 'a life of its own' - a finger that wiggles away all by itself, or perhaps a leg that starts dancing away to some little disco beat that only it can hear. Annoying, but not really alarming. By the time the Tremor becomes alarming, a lot of dopamine-producing cells have died.

Fifty years ago, if you went to the doctor because of your Tremor, or maybe because your walk was becoming shaky or something like that and he diagnosed Parkinson's Disease, you would just have to go home and hope that your family loved you enough to take care of you, because there was absolutely nothing anyone could do. The dopamine-producing cells were dying, and would continue to die. You would get more and more shaky, and then you would get more and more stiff, until eventually you would just be that strange old dear who sits in the armchair by the fire and gets spoon-fed bread-and-milk. It was very sad. But in those days, every family had some old dear in the chair by the fire. I don't think they all had Parkinson's though. Some of them were just very old.

But around that time some scientists began to figure out about the shortage of dopamine in the brain, and started to figure out a way to 'copy' the dopamine molecule and make a form of it that could be gotten into your system through eating it. The early form of it was a powder that you dissolved in water and drank. It tasted foul! So they found a way to make a tablet of it. The idea of this tablet was to replace the dopamine that the brain-cells could no longer make, and in this way relieve the Symptoms of the disease. It was not a medicine to Cure the disease! They could not try to do that because they had absolutely no idea why the brain cells in this part of the brain were dying. In fact, back then they were not even sure that it was dying brain-cells that were causing the disease. So, for the past fifty years or so, Parkinson's disease has been "An Incurable, Progressive, Neurodegenerative condition". In simple terms that means that Parkinson's disease is a disease in which brain-cells are dying and will continue to die and there is nothing we can do about it! We just try to supply enough artificial dopamine to ease the symptoms as much as possible for as long as possible. Depressing, isn't it?!

Ah, but don't despair. If there is one phrase that a scientist can't stand, it is "there-is-nothing-we-can-do-about-it". The boffins have not been idle this past fifty years, and I think they are on the verge of a breakthrough. They are beginning to understand what causes the brain-cells to die. They are very close to figuring out a way to stop them dying. And they are very close to figuring out a way to replace the 'sick' brain-cells with healthy one grown from stem-cells.

Meanwhile, back in our everyday world, what does Parkinson's disease mean now. We no longer have to go sit in the corner, or at least not for many years. We now have tablets to ease and to manage the symptoms caused by the lack of dopamine. But it is not all plain sailing, not all a simple matter of "keep taking the tablets". And this confuses and worries people. We are used to going to the doctor and getting pills, and then getting better. So what is going on here?

Well, the first thing we need to remember is that brain-cells are dying. They just keep on dying, and they don't get replaced. So, the symptoms your doctor prescribes for today are a lot less severe than the symptoms your medicine is trying to treat in three weeks' time. You get so frustrated because you keep taking the tablets and you keep getting worse. And your doctor gets frustrated because he is having to sort of estimate how much worse you are going to get in the near future and prescribe enough to try to keep up with that. He is constantly over-shooting in the hope of hitting a moving target often enough for it to be worth it. And just to really annoy everyone, there is no way to accurately measure how many dopamine-producing brain-cells there are, or how much dopamine they are producing. It all has to be estimated by observing the symptoms shown while you are with the doctor, and your report of the symptoms you experience the rest of the time. This is where medicine becomes an art rather than a science!

The next problem is even more annoying. The doctor prescribes a tablet of a known strength, and you swallow it. But what is unknown, and unknowable, is how much of the dopamine in that tablet will get from your gut into your bloodstream. Not a lot, is the short answer. Most of the dopamine in the tablet ends up in the sewer. (I wonder what effect that is having on the rats?) And as if poor absorbing level was not enough to be thinking about, there is the added complication of competition. You see, for anything to pass from the gut into the blood, it has to be carried by special enzymes. And the enzymes that are capable of carrying dopamine were not designed to carry dopamine. They were designed to carry the proteins from your dinner. And if you give them a choice between picking up a dopamine and picking up a protein, they will pick up the protein. And there goes another bit of your medicine off to the sewers. You can try to minimise this by making sure that you leave a decent gap between eating protein and taking your tablets. But it is not simply a matter of timing. It is a matter of digestion.

The protein from chicken soup will pass through your system a lot faster than the protein from a steak, because the steak needs a lot of digesting to change it from meat to soup inside your tummy. The protein from a small meal will pass through your system faster than the protein from a big meal, simply because your tummy has to work a lot harder to stir about a big meal and mix into it all those amazing digestive juices that turn meat into soup. There are all sorts of other factors that control how fast or how slow the protein is processed; the temperature, the time of day, your mood – all sorts of things. It really is a lottery. One effect of this lottery can be quite surprising. The tablet you take after your breakfast might end up just sitting around in your tummy for hours. And then you take your next dose of tablets, and your tummy decides to process both sets together and fires them off down the line to your gut. All the carriers in the gut are parked at the curb with their engines running, and loads of dopamine gets carried across in one big convoy, and wreaks havoc on your system.

That brings us to one of the biggest problems in treating Parkinson's. The dreaded Side Effects! No dopamine, or lack of dopamine, causes the symptoms of Tremor and Freezing. Freezing is the common name for what the doctors call Bradykinesia. It is a slowing of movement and eventually a complete stopping of movement. Oddly enough, it is a progression of the Tremor. It is a Tremor that has become so fast that no movement is possible and that is why it often hurt like hell. Enough dopamine stops the Tremor, but too much dopamine can cause the Tremor. Catch 22!

Too much dopamine can cause another kind of weird movement – Dyskinesia. This strange writhing, twisting, twitching, movement was the subject of quite some media outrage a few years ago when some idiot mocked Michael J. Fox for it. We call it Dyskie dancing, and try not to worry about it. But it is not all fun and games. Dyskinesia can make it difficult to breathe when it starts up in your rib muscles and it can cause a pain in the neck when your head just won't stop bopping around.

Wow, what fun! You have too little, and then you have too much. You have Freezing, and then you have Dyskinesia. But, with a little bit of careful management, somewhere in there you have times when you have just enough dopamine in your system to be able to live some sort of a normal life. In those times, you have to make sure that you are getting the most out of your life. The doctors are doing everything they can to find the best doses of the best medicines to manage your symptoms. The research scientists are doing everything they can to find out exactly what is causing this disease, and how best to stop it.

So, we just do everything we can to live the best life we possibly can given the state we are in. We love as much as we can, we laugh as much as we can, we appreciate the beauty in the world around us and the kindness and patience of the people around us. And we thank our lucky stars that we were not born fifty years earlier!

Emer Cloherty - 30 January 2018.

The Frozen Mask

Sunset at Mullaghmore, County Sligo.

Conclusion

I hope that these little anecdotes and insights give you a little more understanding of how a disease like Parkinson's can impact a person's life. A sudden life changing event without warning can totally change your health, lifestyle, relationships, and how you view the world.

It comes with "gifts" of pain. Illness, anxiety, depression, fear, and worry. To mention but a few. It robs you of your independence, freedom, your sense of self confidence, and self-esteem. It can be a lonely and frightening place at times. But somehow, we have the strength deep within us, to finally accept and the courage to adapt and to change. To cope with the ever changing challenges and demands our disease has thrust upon us.

I hope through my poetry, I can help to bring a better understanding and you may even enjoy and even dare I say, "inspire" some of you on your journey, whatever troubles and worries you may be carrying on your shoulders!

I would like to thank all who have helped and encouraged me on my journey. For the friends, family, medical team. and especially my wife Emer.

To all those readers for their comments and support and for taking the time to read my work and to contact me.

Glossary

Akinesia: Inability to start movement (Freezing).
Bradykinesia: Slowness of movement.
Dyskinesia: Involuntary movement.
Dystonia: Painful cramps.
Freezing of Gait: Inability to keep continuous movement
 without stopping.
PWPD: Person with Parkinson's Disease.

Acknowledgements

There are a few people I would like to mention and to thank with all my heart, for their support and encouragement in my life with Parkinson's Disease and there are so many people, many of whom are strangers, who by their smile or kind comment, bring a little joy and comfort to my heart.

Parkinson's Association of Ireland - Mayo Branch.
Special Thanks to Caroline McLoughlin and Jacqui McCormack.

Medical Team:
Neurologist - Dr Kevin Murphy and his team.
Parkinson's Specialist Nurse - Gavin Duffy.
The nursing staff at Sligo General Hospital
My G.P Dr T Lynch and all his staff.
Physiotherapists - Donna Kitt and James Diskin of Corrib Physiotherapy.
Pharmacist - All the staff at Wards Chemist, Sligo.
Voice Therapists - Sharon, Claire, and Robin of the HSE.

To friends, family, inlaws, and outlaws! My Facebook friends and followers and to you dear reader for reading my endeavours to capture some of the emotions of an ordinary man trying to cope with and to come to terms with a life changing condition. A disease that is insidious and robbing me of my strength, energy, independence.

And last but not least - my wife Emer for her patience, understanding, encouragement, and Love.
To quote a famous Canadian actor who also has Parkinson's Disease - ((I am) a Lucky Man! Thank you.

About the Author

Born in Cork city, Ireland, I grew up in the Blackrock / Beaumont area and later moved to Midleton. I am presently living in County Sligo with my wife Emer and four cats. Now retired after a successful and fulfilling career as a Travel Consultant and Travel Agency Manager for almost thirty years. With many beautiful memories of people and places. Hobbies and interests include: writing, archaeology, history, philosophy, myths and legends, Science-Fiction, and fantasy. I also like watching sports (with the emphasis on "watching"), including hurling, football, rugby, and quizzes. A mad *Star Trek* fan since the original series in the 1960's, I can also get lost for hours in *The Lord of the Rings* films. I am a Crystal Palace football fan, having followed them since 1969. I hope to have at least another three or four books published before my well runs dry. So, I still have plenty of people to annoy and inflict my poetry on!

When you purchase this book/ebook you will be helping to spread the awareness of Parkinson's Disease. A contribution will be made to the Mayo branch of the Parkinson's Association of Ireland. Thank you.

Made in the USA
Middletown, DE
02 April 2023

27430237R00071